Flip Flops:

A Workbook for Children

Who Have Been

Sexually Abused

FLIP FLOPS:

A Workbook for Children

Who Have Been

Sexually Abused

Phyllis Spinal-Robinson, L.C.S.W.

and

Randi Easton Wickham, L.C.S.W.

Jalice Publishers
Notre Dame, Indiana

FLIP FLOPS:

A WORKBOOK FOR CHILDREN WHO HAVE BEEN SEXUALLY ABUSED.

Published by Jalice Publishers, P.O. Box 455, Notre Dame, IN 46556

First edition published September, 1993. Second printing May, 1994.

———————————————————————

Library of Congress Cataloging-in-Publication Data
Spinal-Robinson, Phyllis and Wickham, Randi Easton.

    Flip Flops: A Workbook for Children Who Have Been Sexually Abused.

    1. Sexually abused children. 2. Incest victims. 3. Mental health — children.
    I. Spinal-Robinson, Phyllis. II. Wickham, Randi Easton. III. Title.

1992

ISBN 0-9627375-3-4

Dedication and Acknowledgements

We would like to dedicate *Flip Flops* to all young children who have been hurt by sexual abuse and who are so very brave and courageous.

We are grateful for the therapists who have believed the children and who are helping them with their healing journeys.

We would like to thank the following:

Our husbands,…Stephen, for his enthusiasm, humor, encouragement, and emotional support…Byron, for loving encouragement and technical computer assistance…Randi's sister, Kelly, for her encouragement, affection, and creativity…Judy Chapperon, an inspiring teacher and mentor for Phyllis…Shahana and Hasina, for their invaluable help with Randi's daughter, Celia, and the household…Randi's niece and nephew, Gabrielle and Eric Easton, for beautiful artwork which is included in this workbook…Phyllis's niece, Marlee Grabiel, for her creative artwork contributions…Michael Hayes, our artist friend, who provided invaluable expertise and assistance…Des Plaines Valley Community Center and our colleagues there, where we've received much of our training and the clinical experience that enabled us to create this workbook…Our publishers and editor for their dedicated commitment in the field of sexual abuse and to this project…and most importantly, our clients who have taught us what bravery truly is.

Introduction For Kids

Dear Kids,

   This workbook has been written especially for you. It will help you and your therapist to talk about the sexual abuse you experienced. It will also help you to understand your feelings. We have talked to a lot of kids who have been sexually abused, and we have found that this workbook can be very helpful. We hope that you will enjoy the activities. They can be very exciting and a lot of fun. If a page is too hard, do the best you can and feel proud of what you've done.

   We hope you learn that you can get help and feel better. Getting to know yourself and learning how to be your own best friend is a very important part of growing up!

                    Yours Truly,

                    Randi & Phyllis

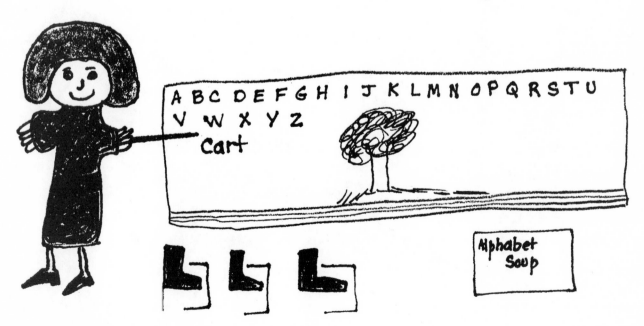

Table Of Contents

Checklist

Most kids who have been sexually abused will have a lot of different thoughts and feelings after the abuse. This is okay. You are not alone in how you feel. It will probably take a while for you to feel okay and safe again. This checklist will help you to know your feelings and thoughts. Put an X by each one that fits you.

Sometimes kids who have been sexually abused...

1. ___Have stomachaches.

2. ___Have bad dreams or nightmares.

3. ___Think that all their friends know what happened.

4. ___Think that no one will like them.

5. ___Feel as if they did something bad.

6. ___Feel mixed up about the person who abused them.

7. ___Have trouble sleeping.

8. ___Were afraid to tell anyone what happened to them.

9. ___Were afraid they'd get punished or get in trouble if they told what happened.

10. ___Have been told something bad will happen to them if they tell.

11. ___Believe that their bodies are ugly or dirty.

12. ___Have problems eating.

13. ___Have a hard time paying attention.

14. ___Have problems in school.

Measuring How You're Doing

This measuring scale will help you to know yourself. It should help you to see what you are thinking and feeling.

Circle one on each line:

I feel scared.	Always	Often	Sometimes	Never
I like myself.	Always	Often	Sometimes	Never
I feel sad.	Always	Often	Sometimes	Never
I'm afraid.	Always	Often	Sometimes	Never
I'm embarrassed.	Always	Often	Sometimes	Never
I feel angry.	Always	Often	Sometimes	Never
I'm happy.	Always	Often	Sometimes	Never
I get mad.	Always	Often	Sometimes	Never
I have nightmares.	Always	Often	Sometimes	Never
I'm shy.	Always	Often	Sometimes	Never
I have friends.	Always	Often	Sometimes	Never
I like other kids.	Always	Often	Sometimes	Never
My family likes me.	Always	Often	Sometimes	Never
I am a good friend.	Always	Often	Sometimes	Never
I'm excited about growing up.	Always	Often	Sometimes	Never

Secrets

A secret is something that someone tells you and asks you not to tell anyone else. There are different kinds of secrets. Some are okay and some are not okay. Usually, secrets that are not okay make you feel uncomfortable or mixed up.

What do you think about the following secrets?
Are they okay or not okay?

<u>Circle okay or not okay</u>

1. A friend tells you about a surprise birthday party. You are asked not to tell.

    okay   *not okay*

2. A friend stole something from the store and asks you not to tell.

    okay   *not okay*

3. Someone you know and trust touches your private parts and asks you not to tell.

    okay   *not okay*

4. Another kid cheats on a test at school. You decide to tell.

    okay   *not okay*

5. Your brother buys a present for your mom and asks you not to tell.

    okay   *not okay*

6. Someone asks you to touch their private parts and asks you not to tell.

    okay   *not okay*

Can you think of some other kinds of secrets? Write them down.
Are these secrets okay or not okay?

_____

_____

_____

_____

_____

_____

_____

_____

Feeling As If The Abuse Was Your Fault

Kids should never be sexually abused! There are many kinds of sexual abuse. If you are mixed up or confused by a touch or by something else that happens to you, talk with your therapist, parent, or someone you trust. Adults should never touch kids in sexual ways. It is wrong, but many kids are sexually abused. Sometimes kids are hurt by adults they trust or by strangers. An adult should never hurt a kid.

NEVER!

Sometimes kids feel that they are to blame for being sexually abused. They may feel that they should have fought back or stopped the abuse. They may feel that it was something bad about them or something they did that caused the abuse. Wrong! Many times kids are confused or afraid to tell about the abuse. For all of these reasons, kids often believe the abuse was their fault. Kids are never to blame for the abuse.

NEVER!

Did you ever think the abuse was your fault?

Tell why.

_____

_____

_____

_____

Who are some people you could talk to about these feelings?

Write their names:

_____

_____

_____

_____

Other Kids' Stories

(If you have trouble reading these stories, ask someone to read them to you.)

1. David, age 8, was often taken care of by John, a friend of his father. David felt that John was a special friend. John often brought David presents, played games with him, and paid attention to him. David felt bad because his father was busy and didn't spend much time with him. David felt very close to John and spent a lot of time with him.

One day, John took David to a park and showed him pictures of people having sex. David was very confused and didn't know what to do. John told him he better not tell because he would get in big trouble. John also gave him a nice present that day, a video game that he had always wanted. David was afraid to tell his parents. He felt ashamed and was afraid that he would get in a lot of trouble if he told anyone what had happened to him. He believed he shouldn't tell because he took the gift.

2. Amy, age 10, was very close with her father. They would often spend time alone. He would tell her that he was lonely and that they had a very "special" relationship. At night while Amy's mother was at work, Amy's father would sexually touch her. Amy was confused and afraid. Amy's father tried to tell her that all fathers taught their daughters this way. Amy believed him, but one day she told her friend Sarah about what happened at home. Sarah told Amy that her father was lying. Amy was very sad. She believed that she couldn't tell a grown up because of all the trouble it could cause; she was afraid it would get her father in trouble or break up the family.

3. Cindy, age 6, liked to play with several kids in the neighborhood. One of her friends, Peter, had an older sister named Sally, age 14. One day while Cindy was at Peter's house, Sally asked her to come into her room so she could show her something. Sally touched Cindy's private parts. Sally told Cindy that she had better not tell anyone because no one would believe her. She also told her she would harm her and her family if she told anyone about what had happened. Sally told her that she had wanted it to happen because she had come into her room. Cindy was very upset and scared. She didn't know what to do.

**Do the stories remind you of anything that happened to you?
Do you feel the kid was ever to blame?**

Please talk with your therapist or a grownup you trust.

You Can Color And Decorate This Page

Sometimes we love people, but we don't like
the things they do to us.

*You can still love people even if you don't like the
things they do to you.*

<u>*Some Facts:*</u>

- *Both boys and girls may be sexually abused.*

- *It's hard for boys and girls to tell anyone about the abuse.*

- *Both males and females may sexually abuse kids.*

- *When kids are abused by their mom or dad, it can be very confusing, especially if the sexual touching felt good.*

- *Kids often feel very confused if the person abusing them is nice to them and asks them to keep this their "special secret."*

Helpful Messages

Here is a list of helpful messages.
Say these messages to yourself or out loud!

1. What happened was not my fault.

2. Adults should never touch kids in a sexual way.

3. I have a right to decide who touches me.

4. There is nothing that I did that made the abuse happen.

5. I am not alone. Other kids have been abused too.

6. People care about me.

7. I care about myself.

8. I believe I can feel better.

Can you make up some helpful messages?

_____

_____

_____

_____

_____

Pick a message for the day. Pick the one that you would most like to hear.

Your Body

Sometimes kids who have been sexually abused have special worries and questions about their bodies. It can help a lot to talk to a parent, teacher, counselor, school nurse, or doctor about these feelings.

Kids sometimes worry that their bodies have been hurt or are different because of the abuse. Also, kids sometimes worry that other people will be able to tell just by looking at them. It is good to talk to an adult about any worries you have.

Your body is good, and it belongs to you. There are some exercises in this book that will help you to get to know your body. It is important to like your body and take good care of it.

What questions or worries do you have about your body?

_____

_____

_____

_____

Remember to talk to someone about these questions or worries.

Your Body

Can you fill in and name the body parts using this picture?

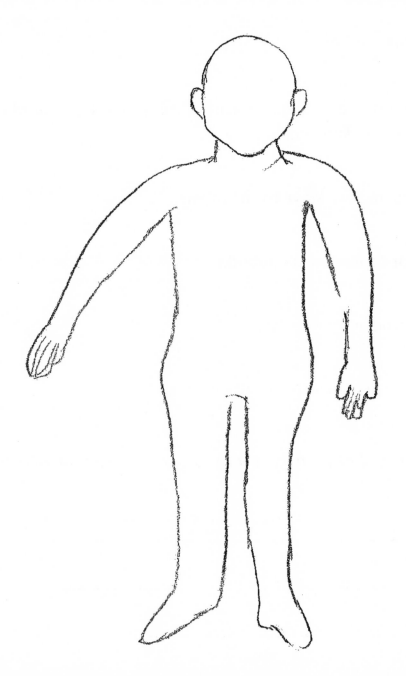

Your body is good. Your body belongs to you. Your body will be healthy and feel good if you treat it with TLC (Tender Loving Care!)

Your Body

Ways to feel good about your body:

1. Do some exercises.

2. Lie down and take some deep breaths to relax you. Feel your breath and picture it relaxing your whole body.

3. Listen to some music. Move to the music.

4. Swim, run, or go for a walk outside.

5. Practice dancing or gymnastics.

6. Play a game such as baseball, soccer, or basketball.

Can you think of other ways that you can take care of your body?

1._____

2._____

3._____

Feelings in Your Body

example: love

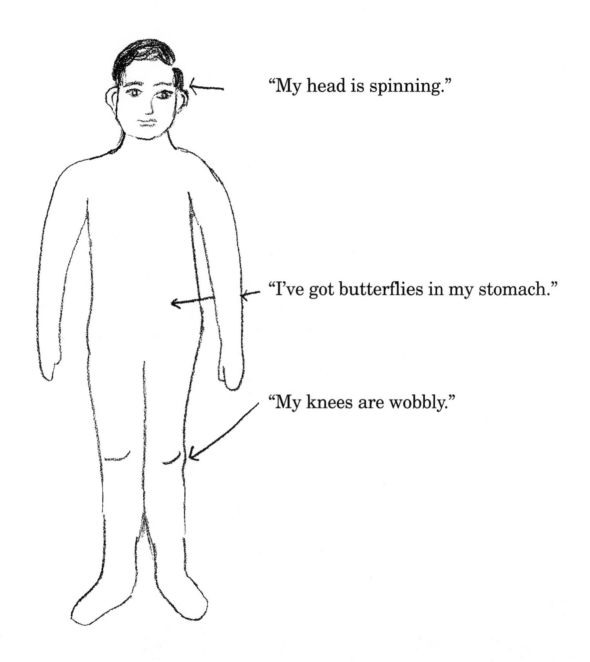

"My head is spinning."

"I've got butterflies in my stomach."

"My knees are wobbly."

People have feelings in their bodies. Can you show on the drawing where you have the following feelings in your body? You can use different colors for different feelings and color them in.

anger   shyness   sadness   fear

surprise   worry   happiness

Kids' Pictures

Learning to Relax

Here is an exercise to practice with your therapist. Once you have learned this exercise, you may wish to do it with a parent, a friend, or alone.

To begin: Get yourself comfortable. Relax, take some
deep breaths, and close your eyes.

Have your therapist or someone else read this to you.

Imagine you are somewhere very beautiful. It may be somewhere you've really been, or it may be a place in your dreams. Is it a forest, a park, or a mountain top? It might be on the beach or at a lake. Maybe it's in the woods somewhere with the smell of pine trees. You pick the place. Are you alone, or is there a pet, a close friend, or someone in your family there with you?

Keep taking deep breaths and relax your whole body. This is a place where you feel relaxed, calm, and safe. It is your place...a place where there are no worries. What are you doing in this place? Are you resting, sitting, or walking? What do you see? Smell? Hear? How do you feel? This is your place...your safe place.

Now that you have found this place, remember you can go there whenever you want.

It is a place for you to relax and feel better!

Anger

Kids usually feel angry after they have been sexually abused. You have a right to be angry. It is okay to be angry, but it is not okay to do something that will hurt you or someone else. It is very important to find safe ways to show your anger.

Safe Ways to Be Angry:

1. **Do an anger dance.**

2. **Punch pillows.**

3. **Hit a punching bag.**

4. **Write a letter telling how angry you are. You may or may not decide to mail it.**

5. **Go for a run or hit a ball against a wall.**

6. **Do a silent scream or scream out loud.**

7. **Talk to your therapist or someone you trust about your anger.**

8. **Make balls out of clay or paper and throw them at a target.**

What are some other ways that you can safely show your anger?

_____

_____

_____

Draw a picture showing how you were sexually abused or how you felt about being sexually abused:

Kids' Letters

Dear Mike,

I hate you for what you did to me. I hope you go to jail.

I miss you. I'm really mad at you. Thank you for the presents you gave me. I hope you're not mad at me.

> Billy

Sometimes kids have both good and bad feelings about the person who abused them. Billy thought Mike was a good friend because he took him places and made him feel special. Billy was hurt and angry about the abuse, but still missed Mike. It's normal and okay to have many feelings at the same time.

JJ- you better not touch my privates any more. you're not supposed to do that. I don't want you doing that to me any more.

Tim

I hate you. I think your a
bum. I really don't like what
you did to me. I don't think
I can forgive you either.

Mary,
I don't like what you
did to me. It makes me
feel mad and sad.
I will never let you
do those sexual things
to me again.
Marie

Write A Letter To The Person Who Abused You

To:_____   Date:_____

From:_____

When you abused me, I felt _____

_____

_____

_____

If you ever try to abuse me again _____

_____

_____

_____

I am safe now because_____

_____

_____

_____

Signed:_____

You may wish to write a letter to another kid who has been sexually abused. What would you say?

For example: You could tell the kid to tell a grown up
and to keep telling people until someone helps.

Date:_____

Dear _____ ,

I know what you are going through is really hard because _____

_____

_____

I wanted to let you know_____

_____

_____

I wanted to let you know that you are not alone and that people care about you. I hope this letter helps you.

Signed:_____

How to Protect Yourself:

Sometimes it is very hard for kids to know when or how to say "no." Kids have a right to say "no."

For example:

Angela would be very uncomfortable each time her mother would insist that she give her Uncle Joe a kiss. Uncle Joe's kisses made her feel strange and funny. Angela told her mother about her feelings. Her mother said she was glad Angela had let her know. She told Angela that she wouldn't make her kiss Uncle Joe or anyone else unless she chose to.

How would you know if someone were talking to you or touching you in a way that made you feel uncomfortable?

_____

_____

Whom would you tell..........................

A. if someone asked you to keep a not okay secret?

_____

_____

B. if someone were talking to you or touching you in a way that made you feel uncomfortable or not okay?

_____

_____

C. if someone ever tries to or does sexually abuse you again?

_____

_____

Your Puppet Show

Materials needed:
brown paper bags,
crayons, pencils, scissors,
and a box to use as a stage

You are the director. You are in charge of the show. Make up who will be the people in your show. Draw and color faces on some brown paper bags and you are ready to go. They can be anyone you want them to be and anything can happen. Act out some scenes. Have one be about what happened to you. You decide what happens when you act it out. You are in charge, but you might wish to have an adult help you.

Draw a picture of the person who abused you.
What would you like to do with this picture?

Kids' Poems

I used to think the
    sky was blue
until I saw the likes of you.
  You used to hold me very tight
    but then you did those
    nasty things at night
I hate the way you touched me.
I hope you fall from a tree.
                    Darlene

I used to trust you
Sometimes you'd let me
Ride in your truck,
I thought I was the one
who had such good luck,
  My friends were jealouse
that I had a friend like you.
Why did you do that to me?
  I don't understand
Why did you hurt me?
                    John

Write Your Own Poem

Draw a Picture of Yourself or Write Some Words Telling About Yourself:

before you were abused

after you were abused

Make Up a Story

Write or tell a story about a kid who has been sexually abused. What kind of ending does your story have?

Date: _____

Title: _____

_____

_____

_____

_____

_____

_____

_____

_____

_____

_____

_____

_____

Getting to Know Yourself

Getting to know yourself can be a lot of fun. It can help you to find things that you enjoy. Let's practice here.

1. What are your favorite colors?

_____

_____

_____

2. What are your favorite foods?

Your least favorite foods?

_____

_____

_____

3. What are your favorite games?

_____

_____

_____

4. What are some things that you like to do?

_____

_____

_____

5. What are some things that you don't like to do?

_____

_____

_____

6. What are some things you like about yourself?

_____

_____

_____

7. Who is your best friend? Tell why...

_____

_____

_____

8. Who are your other friends? Tell why...

_____

_____

_____

Measuring How You're Doing

This measuring scale will help you to know yourself. It should help you to see what you are thinking and feeling.

Circle one on each line:

I feel scared.	Always	Often	Sometimes	Never
I like myself.	Always	Often	Sometimes	Never
I feel sad.	Always	Often	Sometimes	Never
I'm afraid.	Always	Often	Sometimes	Never
I'm embarrassed.	Always	Often	Sometimes	Never
I feel angry.	Always	Often	Sometimes	Never
I'm happy.	Always	Often	Sometimes	Never
I get mad.	Always	Often	Sometimes	Never
I have nightmares.	Always	Often	Sometimes	Never
I'm shy.	Always	Often	Sometimes	Never
I have friends.	Always	Often	Sometimes	Never
I like other kids.	Always	Often	Sometimes	Never
My family likes me.	Always	Often	Sometimes	Never
I am a good friend.	Always	Often	Sometimes	Never
I'm excited about growing up.	Always	Often	Sometimes	Never

A Diary: A Book About Yourself

A diary is a place to write or draw pictures about your thoughts and feelings. It helps you to know yourself! It is a special and private place for you to write and draw. Remember, you are a very special person and there is no one else just like you. You can write or draw anything you want in this diary. You may share some of your diary with other people or you may choose to keep it private. You have a choice.

Begin on the next page by making a cover for your diary.

My Diary

Name:_____

Date:_____

My Diary

Write the date each time you write or draw in your diary.

Date: _____

_____

_____

_____

_____

_____

_____

_____

_____

_____

_____

_____

_____

_____

_____

_____

_____

_____

_____

_____

_____

_____

_____

_____

_____

_____

(You may make a special notebook to use as your diary.)

Imagine

Pretend or imagine that you go to see a fortune teller. Draw a picture
or tell about what your future will look like.

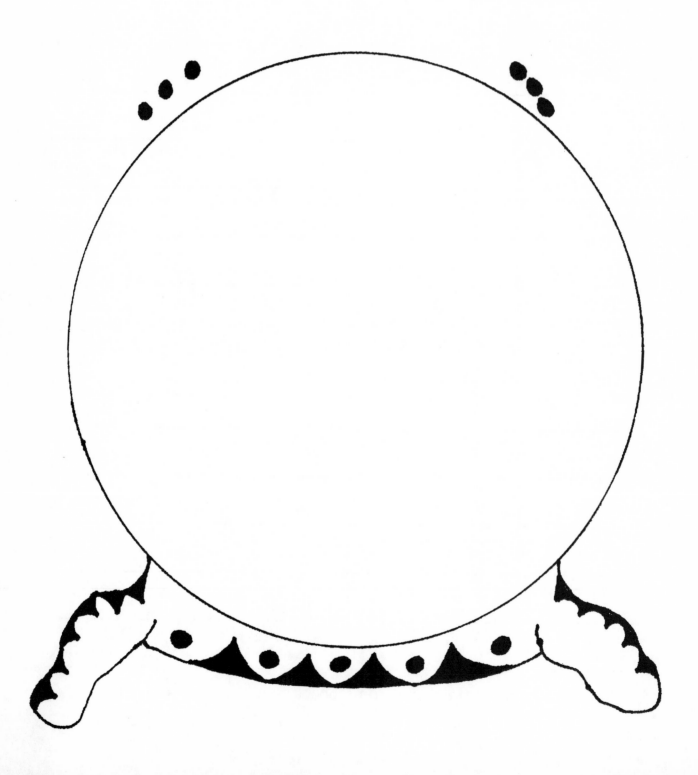

Knowing What You Feel

Everybody has feelings. Feelings are not good or bad. They are not right or wrong. Feelings help you to learn about yourself. It is very important to pay attention to your feelings. Your feelings will help you to decide what you like and what you don't like. Your feelings will help you to know when you are sad, afraid, happy, angry, or lonely. It is very important to know the feelings which are inside of you. It helps to take quiet time to do get to know your feelings.

Color a balloon for each feeling.

Anger

It is okay to be angry. It is also okay to show your anger. It is not okay, though, to hurt yourself or another person when you show your anger.

Some things that make me angry:

1. _____

2. _____

3. _____

4. _____

I show or let out my anger by:

1. _____

2. _____

3. _____

4. _____

Being Hurt and Hurting Others

Sometimes kids who have been sexually abused are confused and angry. They may try to let these feelings out by touching others in sexual ways, hurting others, or hurting themselves.

Here is Anna's story:

Anna's babysitter would always make her take off her clothes and play sexual games. Anna never told anyone because she didn't think they would believe her. Anna felt very mixed up about what had happened to her with the babysitter. She wanted someone else to feel as bad as she had felt. She began making her little brother and sister play the same sexual touching games. Anna was ashamed of how she was acting. Sometimes she would run away from home, and sometimes she would think about hurting herself. Anna finally told her mother about what had happened to her with the babysitter.

What would you tell Anna to do instead of playing the sexual touching games with her brother and sister?

_____

_____

<u>Circle yes or no</u>

Have you ever wanted to break something on purpose?

Yes   No

Have you ever wanted to touch someone in a sexual way?

Yes   No

Have you ever touched someone in a sexual way?

Yes   No

Have you ever wanted to hurt someone else?

Yes   No

Have you ever wanted to hurt yourself?

Yes   No

If you circled yes to any of these questions, talk with your therapist.

Feelings

What are some things that make kids feel:

Happy?

1. _____
2. _____
3. _____

Afraid?

1. _____
2. _____
3. _____

Mad?

1. _____
2. _____
3. _____

Sad?

1. _____
2. _____
3. _____

Excited?

1. _____
2. _____
3. _____

Draw and color a picture of something that makes you happy:

Draw and color a picture of something that makes you sad:

Draw and color a picture of something that makes you angry:

Draw and color a picture of something that would be exciting for you:

Draw and color a picture of something that makes you feel afraid:

Draw and color a picture showing what you could do to help yourself not be afraid:

Feeling Sentences

Finish these sentences:

I like it when _____

I get upset when _____

I feel the best when _____

I am _____

My dad is _____

My mom is _____

My family _____

I don't want to _____

I like myself when _____

I cry when _____

The thing I like most about myself is _____

I get sad when _____

I think I can _____

I know I can _____

My feelings get hurt when _____

Nobody understands that _____

I feel confused when _____

I feel safe when _____

I don't like _____

I have fun when _____

I can _____

My biggest fear is _____

I feel ashamed when _____

When I grow up _____

I'm glad to be me because _____

I am great because _____

Let's Take a Break!

It's important to make time for fun and play activities.

Where can these things be found?

ferris wheel_____carnival_____   drums _____

swimming pool _____   actor _____

toaster _____   flowers _____

radio _____   zebra _____

mirror _____   globe or atlas_____

boat _____   dolphin _____

Can you fill in the blanks to finish these words. These are all zoo animals.

e l e p h a n _   m o n _ e y   l a m _

g i r a f _ e   z _ b r a   s h _ _ p

k o _ l a   b e a r   p e n _ u i n   _ i g e r

w a l r u _   t u r _ l e   l _ _ n

Riddle: Why did the wolf cross the street?

Finding Feelings

Find and circle the words in this feeling puzzle.

Here are the words you can find in the puzzle. The answers to the puzzle are on the next page.

glad   shy   silly   upset   afraid

sad   worried   happy   angry

g l a d o   s i l l y

w o r r i e d A N G R Y

p i s h y   o e   s a d

t o u p s e t   z

x s p h a p p y   n   l

n a f r a i d

If you can't find all the words, ask someone for help.

Answers to Finding Feelings

g l a d o   s i l l y

w o r r i e d A N G R Y

p i s h y   o e   s a d

t o u p s e t   z

x s p h a p p y   n l

n a f r a i d

You are not alone.

You can always ask for help.

Feelings

Sometimes you will have more than one feeling at the same time. Maybe someone close to you will do something that upsets you or hurts you. You may feel confused because you love or care about that person, but what he or she did caused you to be angry or hurt. It's okay to have more than one feeling at a time. Don't try to push feelings down or pretend that you don't have them. Pay attention to your feelings. They are very important.

In each of these stories, the kid has more than one feeling at the same time.

Story 1.

Katie's mom and dad were getting divorced. She loved both of her parents very much. She also felt as if she were in the middle and didn't want to have to choose between them. Katie felt very sad about the divorce. She also felt angry because her parents couldn't work things out. Sometimes she worried that it was her fault that they were splitting up.

Can you think of other feelings Katie might have had? Write down the different feelings Katie had about her parents' divorce.

_____

_____

_____

_____

Story 2.

Jimmy liked his uncle Mike very much. Uncle Mike took him to fun places, bought him things, and let him stay at his house for overnights. Jimmy felt very special to his uncle Mike. Sometimes Uncle Mike played a game that made Jimmy feel funny. He would touch private parts of Jimmy's body and ask Jimmy to touch private parts of his body. He told Jimmy that the touching game would be their special secret. This made Jimmy feel confused. He loved his uncle Mike, but he didn't like the touching game.

What else do you think Jimmy might have felt? Write down the different feelings Jimmy had about his being sexually abused.

_____

_____

_____

Can you think of a time when you had more than one feeling at a time? Write or draw a picture about this time.

_____

_____

_____

_____

A Feeling Exercise

1. What are some things that make you feel upset?

_____

_____

_____

_____

2. Name some things that make you feel happy.

_____

_____

_____

_____

3. What kinds of things make you feel angry?

_____

_____

_____

_____

4. Name some people who help you to feel happy. What do they do that helps you to feel happy?

_____

_____

_____

_____

5. Draw a picture about a nightmare or something that scares you.

6. What are some things that you could do to protect yourself or to feel less scared?

_____

_____

_____

_____

_____

_____

_____

_____

Feelings: Can you match the feeling word with the action? Each answer should be used only once.

Happy _____   A. Sitting by yourself in a corner.

Angry _____   B. Having tears fill your eyes.

Sad _____   C. Feeling nervous and not talking to new
                           people.

Scared_____   D. Kicking a tree.

Lonely_____   E. Laughing or giggling.

Shy _____   F. Hiding somewhere.

Answers
1. E
2. D
3. B
4. F
5. A
6. C

Meet My Family

These are the people in my family:

Tell something about your family.

_____

_____

_____

What are some things about your family that make you feel good?

_____

_____

_____

What are some things about your family that make you feel sad?

_____

_____

_____

Name a person you talk to when you are upset, sad, or afraid.
Why this person?

_____

_____

_____

_____

What would you like to say to your family?

_____

_____

_____

_____

What else would you like to say about your family?

_____

_____

_____

_____

What Do You Dream About At Night?

Draw and color a picture or write some words about your dreams.

Feeling Good About Myself

Ways I can take care of myself:

1. Talk to my family or a friend.

2. Give myself a hug.

3. Get a hug from someone I care about.

4. Take a walk by myself or with a friend.

5. Read a good book.

6. Write or draw in my diary.

7. Write a story, draw a picture, sing a song, or write a poem.

8. Play with a pet.

9. Watch a movie.

Add things that you enjoy doing!

_____

_____

_____

_____

Wishes

1.

2.

3.

Make 3 wishes on this special lantern!

Daily Schedule

Sometimes it helps to make plans for things you would like to do. Here is one kid's plan. On the bottom half of the page, you can make up one of your own.

Things to do today

Day of the week: Thursday

Go to school.

Go to baseball practice.

Go to therapy.

Do my homework.

Have dinner.

Call my friend Tom.

Take a bath.

Go to bed.

_____

Can you make up your own plan?

Things to do today

Day of the week:_____

_____

_____

_____

_____

Name Plate

Print your name and make a design out of it.

How I Feel About Myself:

Make a list of the things you like about yourself.

Examples: I'm a good friend.

I'm funny.

_____

_____

_____

_____

_____

_____

_____

Make a list of the things you can do well.

Examples: I'm a good roller skater.

I'm a good baseball player.

_____

_____

_____

_____

_____

_____

_____

Thinking About Yourself

Pick some words that tell what you are like. Put a word that says something about you in each of the circles below. Next, color in the space around the circles and make a design.

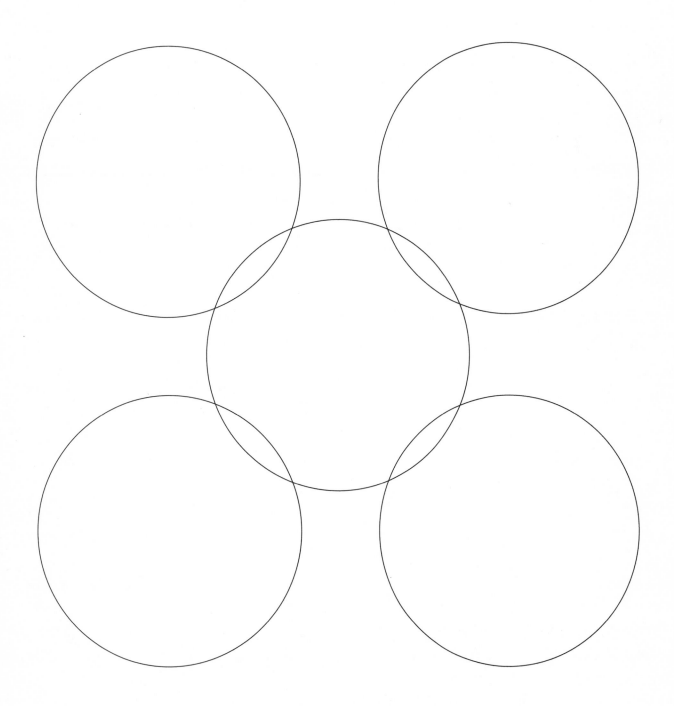

An Art Project For You

Cut out some magazine pictures that tell something about you, and paste them here to make your own picture. You can add words to the picture, too. Have fun!

Art Gallery

Draw a picture of yourself or put your photograph here.

Picture of:_____

(Your Name)